AMAZING CREATURES

by

Rebecca L. Grambo

Copyright © 2004, 2006
Learning Challenge, Inc.
www.learningchallenge.com

Manufactured in China

0706-3C

Contents

Photo Credits

R. E. Barber: pages 17, 26-27, 30
Bill Beatty: page 31
Cathy & Gordon Illg: page 11
Gary Kramer: page 16
Dwight Kuhn: page 12
Tom & Pat Leeson: pages 10, 26
Robert & Linda Mitchell: pages 8, 21
Norbert Wu: page 24
Denis Paquin/AP Photo: page 18
Tom Brakefield/DRK: pages 8-9, 20-21, 24-25
M. C. Chamberlain/DRK: page 29
Marty Codano/DRK: page 14
Chuck Dresner/DRK: page 27
Michael Fogden/DRK: pages 9, 13, 27
Stephen J. Krasemann/DRK: page 20
Dwight Kuhn/DRK: page 30
C. C. Lockwood/DRK: page 28
S. Nielson/DRK: page 23
Doug Perrine/DRK: page 11
Leonard Lee Rue III/DRK: pages 22-23
Anup Shah/DRK: page 25
Jeremy Woodhouse/DRK: page 22
Norbert Wu/DRK: page 28
George Grall/National Geographic Society: page 31
Robert F. Sisson/National Geographic Society: page 15
A. J. Copley/Visuals Unlimited: page 13
Dave B. Fleetham/Visuals Unlimited: page 25
A. Kerstitch/Visuals Unlimited: pages 28-29
Ken Lucas/Visuals Unlimited: page 19
Joe McDonald/Visuals Unlimited: page 12
Glenn M. Oliver/Visuals Unlimited: pages 16-17
Science VU/Visuals Unlimited: page 16
Stephen Frink/Waterhouse: page 14
HPH Photography/The Wildlife Collection: pages 14-15
Chris Huss/The Wildlife Collection: page 21
Tom Vezo/The Wildlife Collection: pages 11, 23

Cover Photo: Tom & Pat Leeson
Endpages (front): Anup Shah/DRK
Endpages (back): Dan Nedrelo

Illustration Credit

Howard S. Friedman: page 18

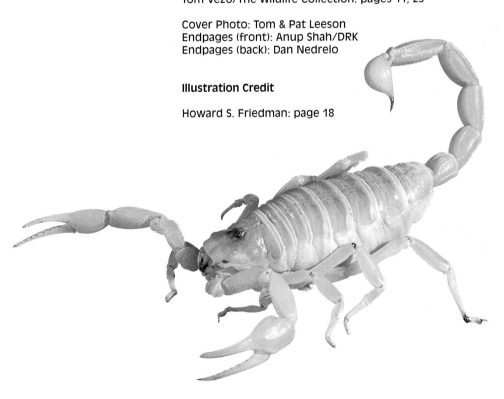

CLAWS
AND JAWS

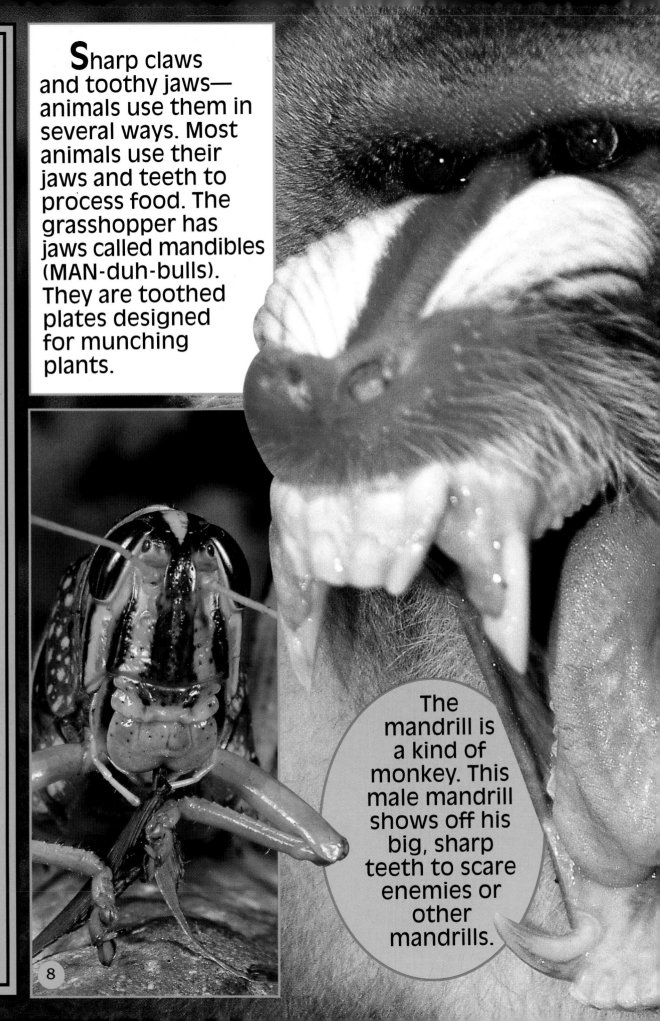

CLAWING AND JAWING

Sharp claws and toothy jaws—animals use them in several ways. Most animals use their jaws and teeth to process food. The grasshopper has jaws called mandibles (MAN-duh-bulls). They are toothed plates designed for munching plants.

The mandrill is a kind of monkey. This male mandrill shows off his big, sharp teeth to scare enemies or other mandrills.

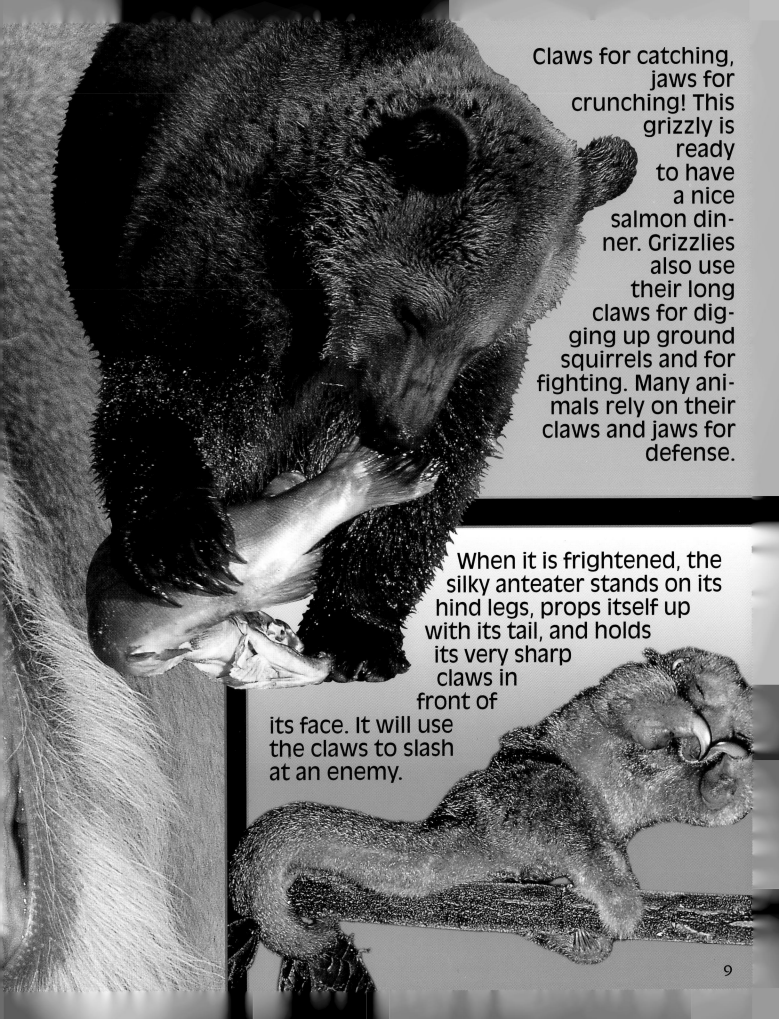

Claws for catching, jaws for crunching! This grizzly is ready to have a nice salmon dinner. Grizzlies also use their long claws for digging up ground squirrels and for fighting. Many animals rely on their claws and jaws for defense.

When it is frightened, the silky anteater stands on its hind legs, props itself up with its tail, and holds its very sharp claws in front of its face. It will use the claws to slash at an enemy.

9

YOU ARE WHAT YOU EAT!

An animal's jaws and teeth are built for a specialized diet. Animals that hunt other animals are called carnivores (CAR-nuh-vorz). Carnivores need sharp, strong teeth to catch and kill their prey. The long, pointed fangs in this wolf's mouth are called canines (KAY-nines). Most carnivores have big canines.

The upper jaws of certain kinds of whales have big plates of a bristly material called baleen (buh-LEEN). The whales feed by taking a big gulp of water, then forcing the water out through the baleen. The bristles trap even the tiniest food, which the whale swallows. Baleen whales can eat as much as two and a half tons a day!

Deer have no front teeth on top, and the ones on the bottom are quite small. A deer uses the big flat teeth along the sides of its jaws to grind up the plant food that it eats.

Rodents like this coypu (KOY-poo) have long front teeth called incisors (in-SIGH-zurs). The incisors never stop growing. Because rodents chew a lot, their incisors stay very sharp. That means rodents can eat hard foods, such as nuts and seeds.

11

FANGS-A-LOT

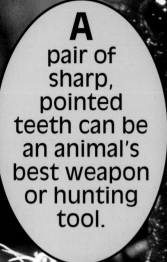

A pair of sharp, pointed teeth can be an animal's best weapon or hunting tool.

As the jumping spider leaps, its jaws open wide and huge fangs unfold from each end. When the spider lands on its prey, it is ready to bite.

A snake's fangs fold up against the roof of its mouth until needed. They work like a hollow needle, injecting poison into prey. Some snakes have fangs nearly two inches long!

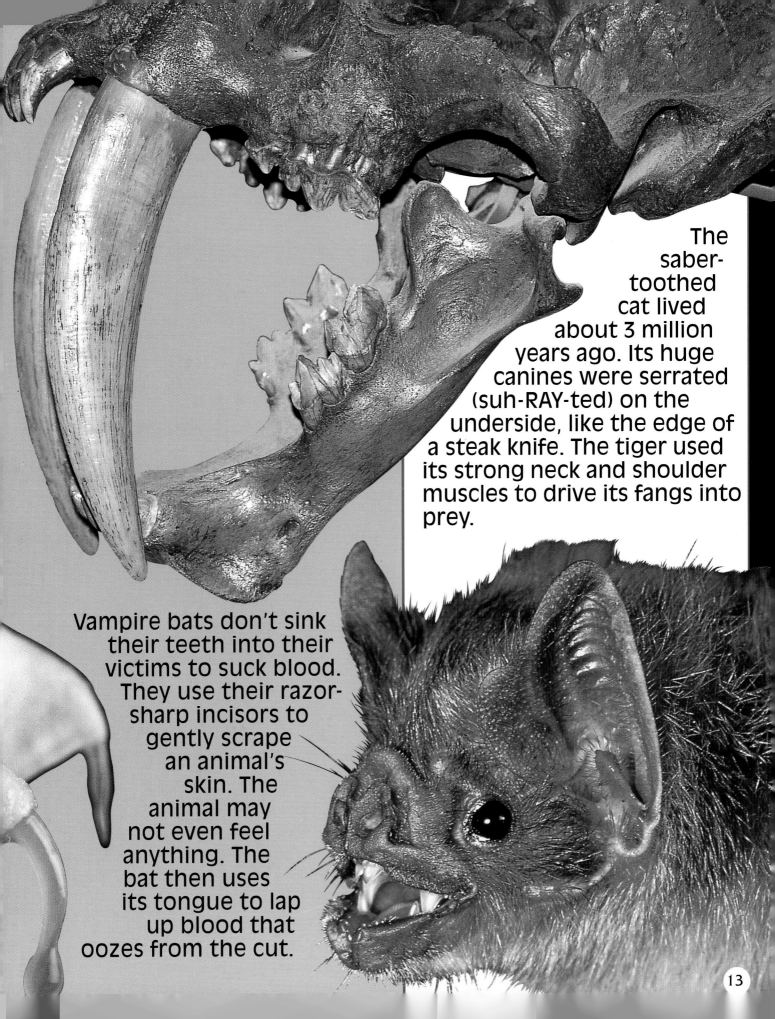

The saber-toothed cat lived about 3 million years ago. Its huge canines were serrated (suh-RAY-ted) on the underside, like the edge of a steak knife. The tiger used its strong neck and shoulder muscles to drive its fangs into prey.

Vampire bats don't sink their teeth into their victims to suck blood. They use their razor-sharp incisors to gently scrape an animal's skin. The animal may not even feel anything. The bat then uses its tongue to lap up blood that oozes from the cut.

MORE THAN CLAWS

Sometimes claws have added features for helping animals catch or eat food.

The scorpion has tiny hairs on its claws that sense movement in the air. Then the scorpion grabs and stings its victim.

Underneath the horseshoe crab is a mass of legs. The legs end in claws that work like jaws, catching clams and worms. Then these "claw jaws" grind up the food before the horseshoe takes a mouthful.

14

The five-inch-long mantis shrimp is armed and dangerous. Its claws fold up like knife blades. But it can snap them out in a flash to spear or club its food. Sometimes it even attacks other mantis shrimps.

Waving its oversized claw in the air, a male fiddler crab signals to females nearby. It also uses the big claw to defend its home. The really important job of gathering up food is done by the crab's small claw.

TUSK TUSK TUSK!

Some teeth called tusks are very, very long! The narwhal (NAR-wall) is a whale that lives in northern oceans. Male narwhals have a single ivory tusk that can grow to be almost 10 feet long.

Both the upper and lower canines of a warthog grow up and out to form tusks. Warthogs are plant-eaters. They would rather run than fight. But when they have to fight, they use their tusks to defend themselves.

The canine teeth of a walrus grow into tusks that may be almost three feet long. The walrus uses its tusks for digging up shellfish and to help pull itself onto shore. Walruses also use their tusks when they fight.

Both male and female African elephants grow tusks. These big front teeth can be over 11 feet long and weigh more than 200 pounds each, but most are smaller. The big tusks aren't as important to the elephant as its smaller, grinding teeth. It needs those teeth to eat properly.

17

DINO MIGHT!

Dinosaurs had bigger claws and jaws than those of any animal living today. Carcharodontosaurus (KAR-kar-uh-DON-toh-SORE-us) had eight-inch teeth in its six-foot-long head.

Tyrannosaurus (tuh-RAN-uh-SORE-us) was built for eating meat. Designed for biting and tearing flesh, the teeth in this dino's four-foot skull were about six inches long and sharp as knives.

18

Deinonychus (die-NON-ick-us) was only about four feet tall. But it had a huge five-inch claw on its second toe. When Deinonychus ran, the claw folded up to stay out of the way. The claw moved into position for kicking and slashing when Deinonychus attacked its prey.

DIG THIS

Some animals have claws made for digging and shoveling.

The badger's strong legs end in big claws, which are used to dig up small animals to eat. A badger can dig faster in loose dirt than a person can with a shovel.

20

Moles have paddle-shaped front paws that end in sharp claws. They have ridges on their front toes that help them move dirt. Moles dig by "swimming" through the dirt, first using one paw, then the other.

The mole cricket lives like a mole. The cricket's sharp claws and bristles on its legs help it move through the soil.

Giant anteaters use their two long, sharp, curved claws to rip into termite mounds. The mounds may be as hard as concrete, but that doesn't stop the anteater.

BIRD BITS

Birds have claws and jaws to fit their lifestyles.

This osprey (AHS-pree) will use its hooked beak to rip off pieces of fish for its dinner. But it is the osprey's sharp claws that grab and hang on to a squirming catch.

They're not really teeth. But a penguin has pointy, spiny bristles on its tongue and in its mouth. Directed toward the back of the mouth, these bristles keep slippery fish from escaping.

22

Woodpecker feet have two toes facing forward, and two pointing to the back. Along with its stiff tail, its toes help the woodpecker balance safely on the side of trees. Then the bird can use its strong bill to poke around in the bark for insects.

Herons eat fish. To catch them, the heron stabs the fish with its sharp bill, which sometimes goes right through the fish. Herons also have a special, flattened claw on one of their toes. They use it for combing through their feathers.

23

SCARY JAWS

The great white shark's mouth is full of sharp teeth. Like other sharks, its teeth grow in rows, one row behind the other. The teeth aren't hooked to the shark's jaw, but grow out of the skin. When the teeth in the first row wear out, they drop out. The teeth behind them move forward. Over ten years' time, a shark may go through more than 20,000 teeth.

Some animals have a mouth that looks frightening, but these scary jaws do important jobs for the animals.

A roaring lion gives us a good look at his teeth. Hunting cats like lions have very large, sharp canines. Lions use both their claws and jaws to capture and kill their food.

Crocodiles don't have lips, their teeth show, and their mouth leaks even when closed. Even with all those teeth, crocodiles can't chew. They just gulp their food down in big chunks. But those big jaws are very good for grabbing prey.

Moray eels have long, thin teeth designed for catching and holding small prey. Their biggest teeth are hinged, folding back to make it easier for the eels' lunch to slide on by.

GET A GRIP

Claws help animals to catch food, grip tree limbs, and defend themselves.

Animals that spend some or all of their time in trees need their claws to keep them from falling. Babies like this raccoon learn right away how to hang on.

Just like a house cat, the mountain lion keeps its claws tucked in so they stay sharp. When it wants to fight, climb, or catch prey, the big cat extends its claws. This mountain lion is sharpening its claws on a tree.

26

Without its claws, the sloth wouldn't be able to hang around. It spends its life climbing or hanging upside down, with its strong claws hooked over branches. The sloth also uses its claws to pull off leaves to eat.

Bird legs are designed so that the toes tighten around a perch when the bird lands. That's why birds don't fall off their branches when they sleep.

27

INCREDIBLE JAWS

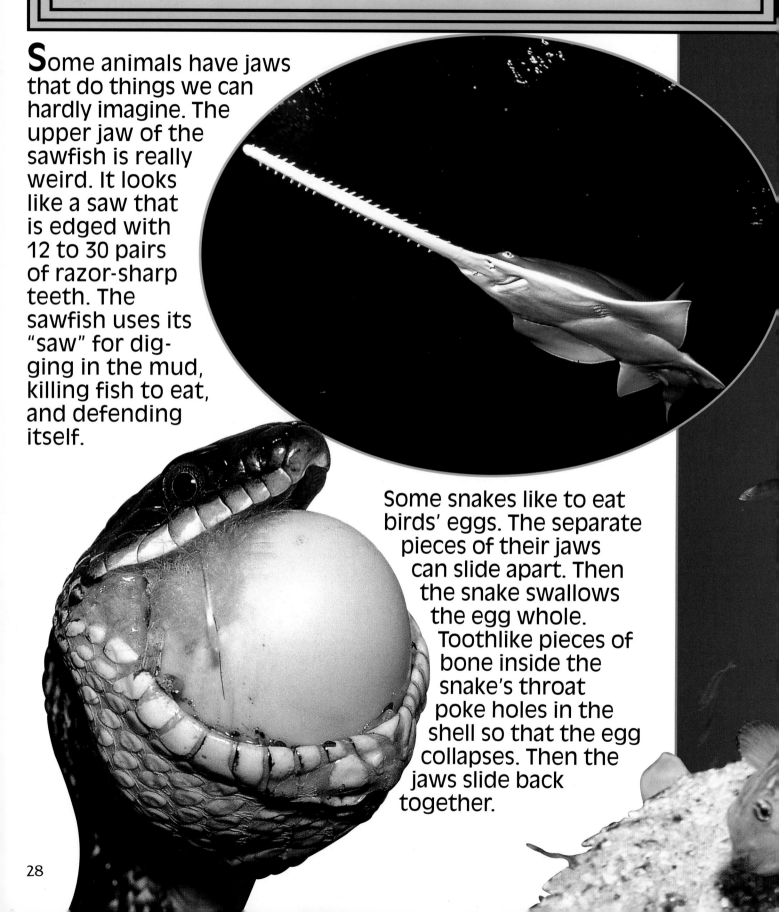

Some animals have jaws that do things we can hardly imagine. The upper jaw of the sawfish is really weird. It looks like a saw that is edged with 12 to 30 pairs of razor-sharp teeth. The sawfish uses its "saw" for digging in the mud, killing fish to eat, and defending itself.

Some snakes like to eat birds' eggs. The separate pieces of their jaws can slide apart. Then the snake swallows the egg whole. Toothlike pieces of bone inside the snake's throat poke holes in the shell so that the egg collapses. Then the jaws slide back together.

The jaws of a whale shark have thousands of teeth and are wide enough to swallow two people. But don't worry. The whale shark eats only small fish and shrimp—lots of them! Its teeth are tiny—much smaller than yours.

The cone shell does its hunting with only one tooth. The tooth may be almost half an inch long. It is thin and hollow. The cone shell fires the tooth into its prey like a harpoon. Then the cone shell's strong poison paralyzes the prey.

BUG BITES

In the insect world, claws and jaws come in strange shapes. The "horns" on this male stag beetle are really just overgrown jaws. The beetle uses them for attracting a mate or for fighting with other males, but not for eating.

Dragonflies live underwater for a while before they grow wings. Young dragonflies are called nymphs (NIMFS). Nymphs have jaws that fold up over their face like a mask. They can unfold them quickly to catch prey.

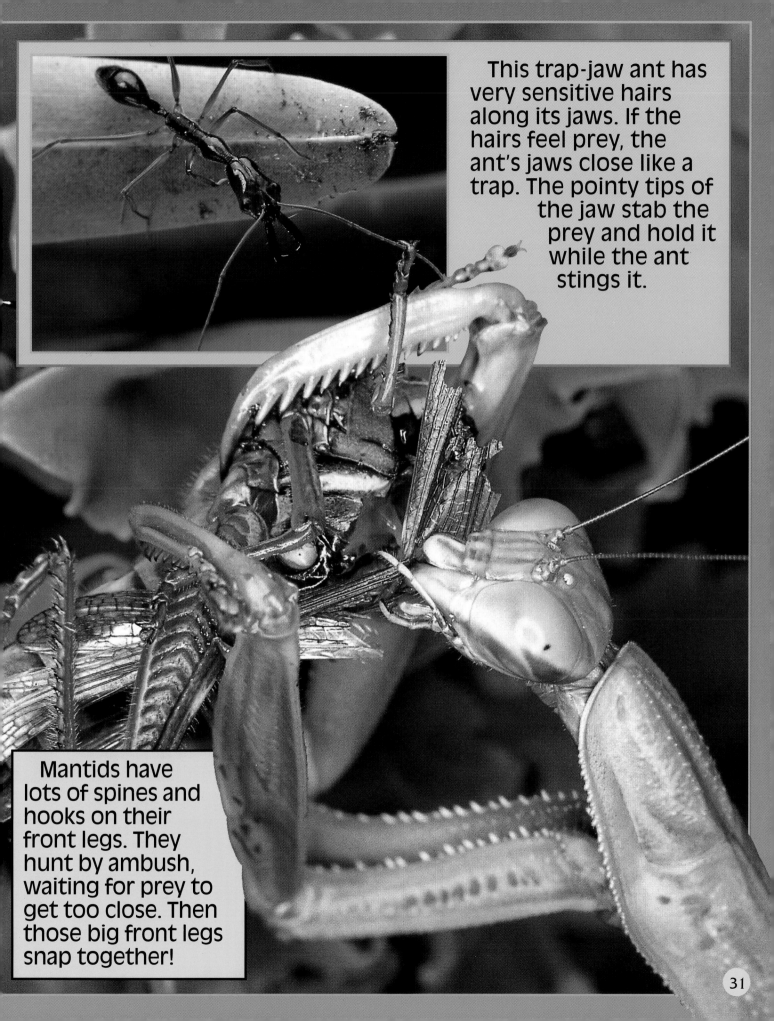

This trap-jaw ant has very sensitive hairs along its jaws. If the hairs feel prey, the ant's jaws close like a trap. The pointy tips of the jaw stab the prey and hold it while the ant stings it.

Mantids have lots of spines and hooks on their front legs. They hunt by ambush, waiting for prey to get too close. Then those big front legs snap together!

Photo Credits

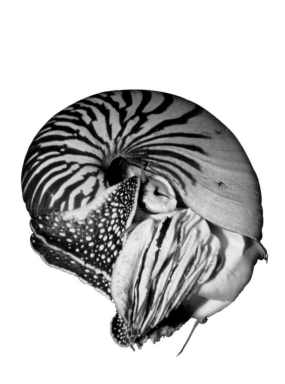

EYES

ANIMAL EYES

Every day our eyes tell us things about the world around us. We see the color and shape of objects. Then we use those clues to figure out what the object is. We may be able to tell whether it is hot or cold, or if it's rough or smooth. We can tell which objects are moving and if they are moving toward us. We do all of this without really thinking about it.

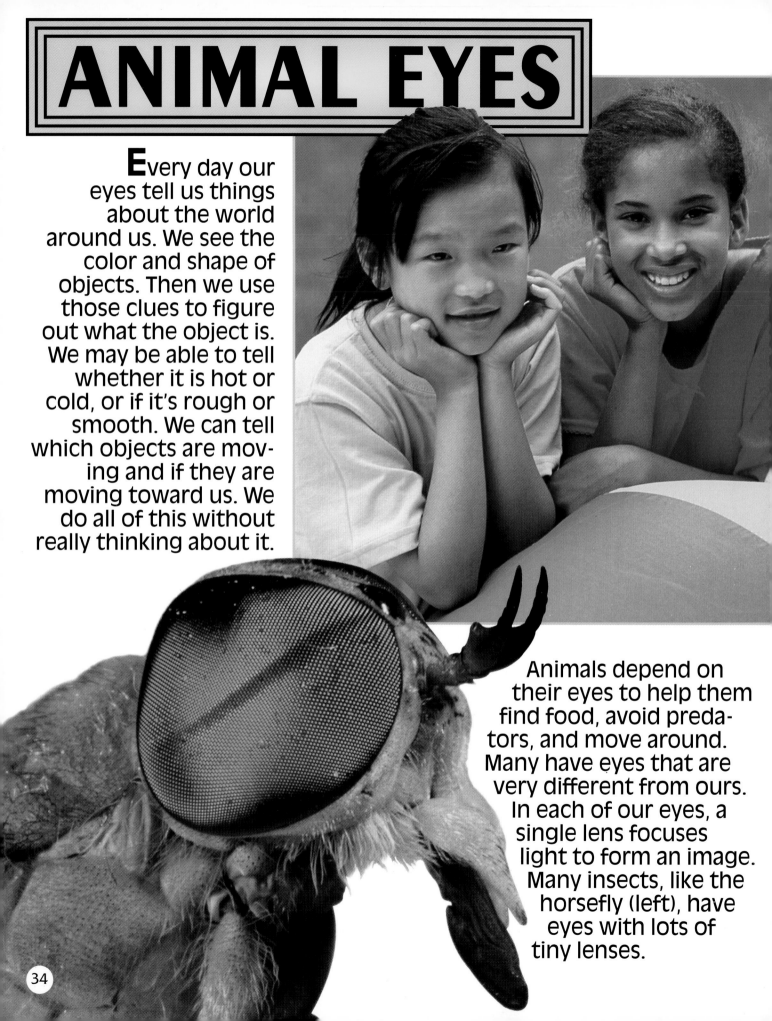

Animals depend on their eyes to help them find food, avoid predators, and move around. Many have eyes that are very different from ours. In each of our eyes, a single lens focuses light to form an image. Many insects, like the horsefly (left), have eyes with lots of tiny lenses.

A scallop may have as many as 100 tiny eyes. They are scattered in the fringe of tentacles around the shell. Each eye is only about the thickness of a dime! Scallop eyes don't form clear pictures, but they are very good at seeing movement. When a scallop sees a predator coming toward it, the scallop snaps its shell shut!

Most spiders have six or eight eyes. The wolf spider uses all eight of its eyes to hunt for prey. The small eyes on the sides of its head spot movement. Then the spider turns to face its prey so that it can focus with its main eyes and pounce.

IN THE DARK

People are busiest during the day. But many animals are *nocturnal* (nock-TUR-nul), meaning they are most active at night. Special eyes help these animals see in the dark.

Cats have a reflecting layer inside their eyes. The layer bounces light back to the part of the eye where images are formed. This allows cats to use small amounts of light to see in the dark. The reflection also causes the glow in a cat's eyes.

The eyes of many nocturnal animals seem very large compared to the rest of their face. The galago, from Africa, has eyes that make the most of the night's light.

At the center of our eyes, and the eyes of many animals, are small dark openings called *pupils*. They control how much light gets into the eye. Pupils open wide in the dark and close tightly in bright light. Nocturnal animals have very sensitive eyes. They need pupils that can shut tightly during the day. The long, slit pupils of these tree frogs block out bright daylight that could hurt their eyes.

EYES OF THE HUNTER

Our eyes are close together in the front of our head. Cover one eye, then the other. What you see with your right eye overlaps what you see with your left eye. Your brain combines these two images into a three–dimensional picture. This lets you judge how far you are from the objects you are seeing. This is called *binocular* (by–NOK–you–ler) vision. Predators like the wolf, who hunt other animals, usually have eyes positioned in the same way as ours.

A cougar uses sight more than its other senses to find food. Once it spots prey, the cougar sneaks closer until it is near enough to attack. Then the cougar's keen vision helps it to time its pounce correctly.

An eagle's eyesight may be as much as eight times better than ours. That means an eagle soaring above a mountain valley may be able to see a rabbit from up to two miles away!

Owls are nocturnal animals that hunt mostly at night and see very well in low light. Owls use their binocular vision to find a scurrying mouse and then— SWOOP!

LOOK OUT!

Some animals are often hunted for food by other animals. To avoid being eaten, these prey animals need to be constantly aware of what's happening around them.

The large eyes of the prairie dog and the deer are placed on the sides of their head. This makes them very good at spotting even slight movement off to the side. They can see approaching predators in time to run away.

40

The eyes of a bittern are positioned very far apart. To have binocular front vision, the bittern has to point its beak up and look out from underneath it. Another bird, the snipe, has eyes placed way back. It actually has binocular vision behind its head!

Members of the rabbit and hare families can see almost directly behind them. This can be dangerous because it creates a blind spot directly in front of them. One hare was seen running over a cliff because it was so busy watching the predator chasing it!

BUG-EYED

Many insect eyes have lots of tiny lenses called *facets* (FAH–sets). This kind of eye is called a *compound* eye. Compound eyes look very different from our eyes, and they don't form images the same way our eyes do.

Have you ever tried to swat a fly and missed? Compound eyes like those of this robber fly are much better than ours at noticing motion. The fly sees the swatter coming in plenty of time to get out of the way!

The praying mantis is a fierce hunter of other insects. It sees very well, but only within a short distance. Our eyes adjust to focus on distant objects. If an insect with compound eyes wants a better look at something far away, the insect has to move closer.

A dragonfly's eye may have 28,000 to 30,000 facets! Each facet sends back its view of the surrounding scene. The dragonfly sees a picture that is sharp in all directions. Dragonflies have some of the best overall eyesight in the animal kingdom.

UNDER THE SEA

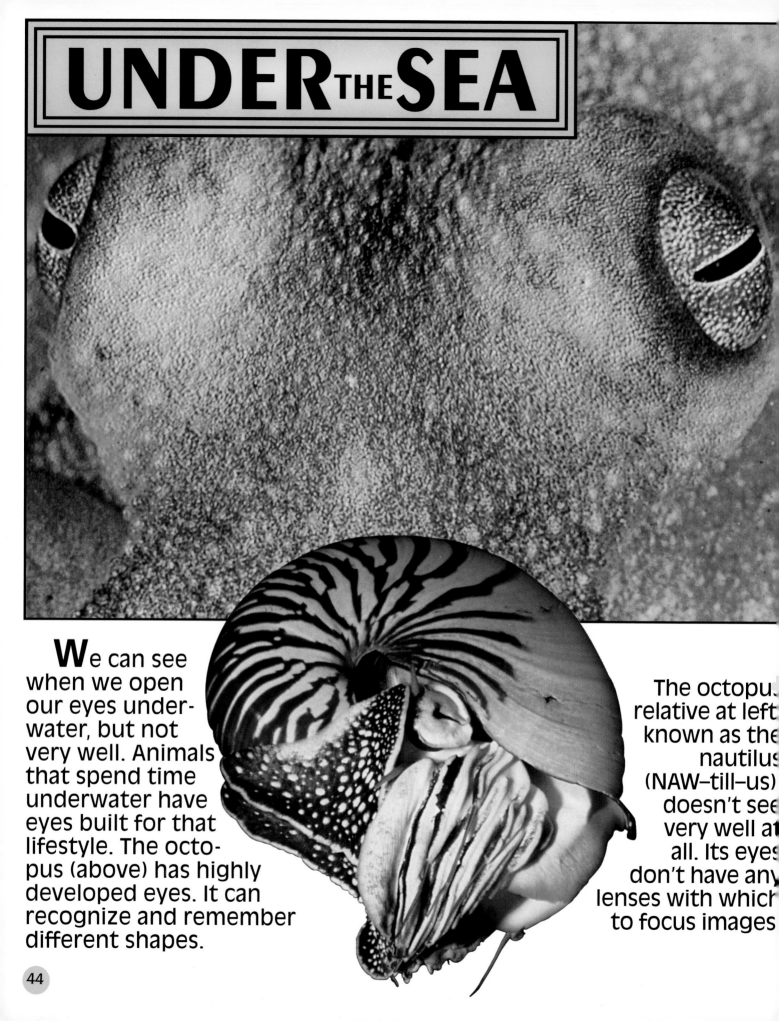

We can see when we open our eyes underwater, but not very well. Animals that spend time underwater have eyes built for that lifestyle. The octopus (above) has highly developed eyes. It can recognize and remember different shapes.

The octopus relative at left, known as the nautilus (NAW–till–us) doesn't see very well at all. Its eyes don't have any lenses with which to focus images.

Penguins spend much of their time underwater. They see better there than on land. Penguins also have a special third eyelid that covers their eyes when they dive. It protects their eyes and still lets them see the fish they're chasing.

The eyes of the hammerhead shark, as well as its nostrils, are located on the ends of its strangely shaped head. No one knows why. These sharks see well to the sides but have a large blind spot directly in front of them. To see ahead, a hammerhead must swing its head back and forth.

PUT A LID ON IT!

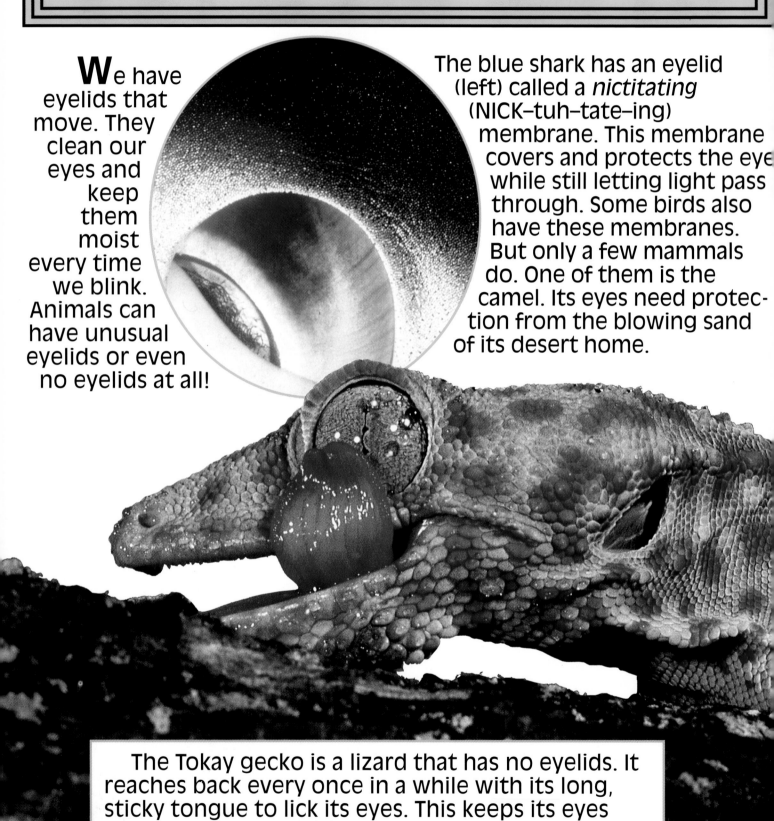

We have eyelids that move. They clean our eyes and keep them moist every time we blink. Animals can have unusual eyelids or even no eyelids at all!

The blue shark has an eyelid (left) called a *nictitating* (NICK–tuh–tate–ing) membrane. This membrane covers and protects the eye while still letting light pass through. Some birds also have these membranes. But only a few mammals do. One of them is the camel. Its eyes need protection from the blowing sand of its desert home.

The Tokay gecko is a lizard that has no eyelids. It reaches back every once in a while with its long, sticky tongue to lick its eyes. This keeps its eyes from drying out and removes dust.

When the sun is very bright, seeing can be difficult. This is a special problem for insects with big eyes and no eyelids. Some insects, like the butterfly at left, have hairs growing in their compound eyes. Scientists think the hairs may help to reduce glare—the same thing sunglasses do for people!

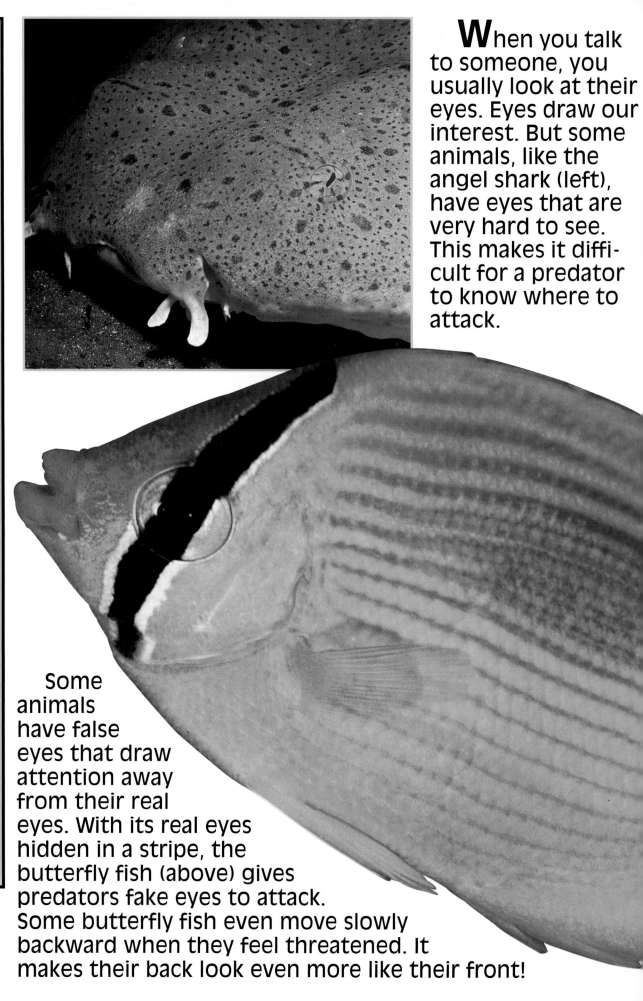

When you talk to someone, you usually look at their eyes. Eyes draw our interest. But some animals, like the angel shark (left), have eyes that are very hard to see. This makes it difficult for a predator to know where to attack.

Some animals have false eyes that draw attention away from their real eyes. With its real eyes hidden in a stripe, the butterfly fish (above) gives predators fake eyes to attack. Some butterfly fish even move slowly backward when they feel threatened. It makes their back look even more like their front!

The emperor moth suddenly opens its wings to show false eyespots. This might scare or puzzle a predator.

The eyespots on the rear end of this caterpillar certainly might confuse an attacking bird. The spots also draw attention away from the caterpillar's head.

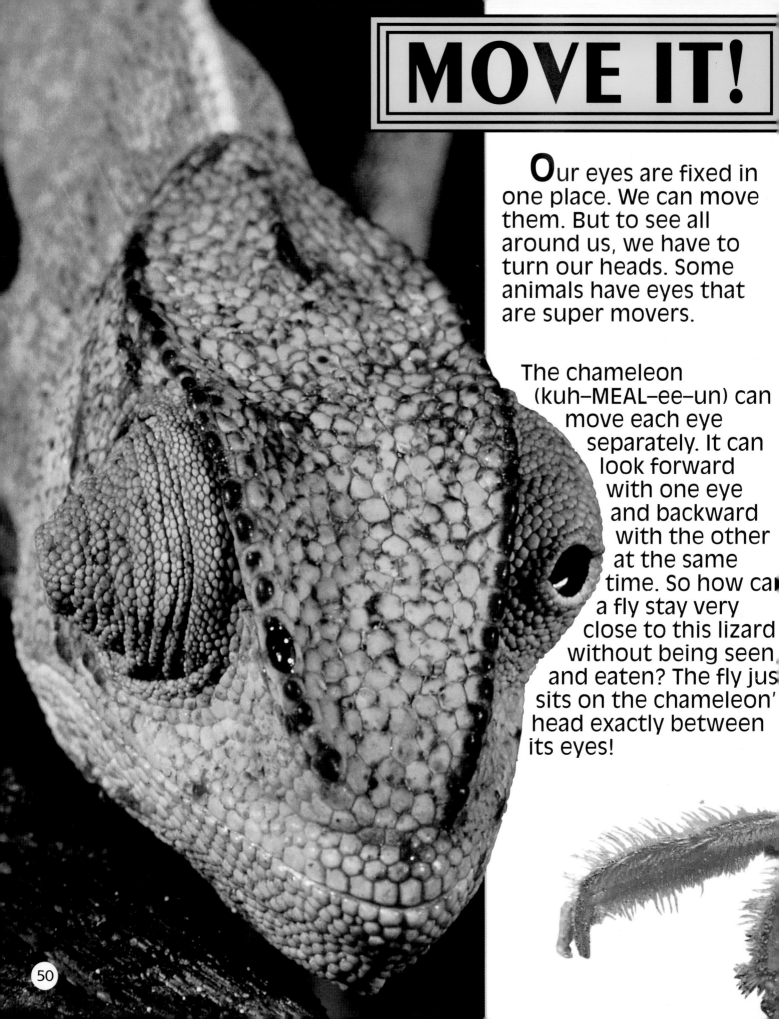

MOVE IT!

Our eyes are fixed in one place. We can move them. But to see all around us, we have to turn our heads. Some animals have eyes that are super movers.

The chameleon (kuh–MEAL–ee–un) can move each eye separately. It can look forward with one eye and backward with the other at the same time. So how can a fly stay very close to this lizard without being seen and eaten? The fly just sits on the chameleon's head exactly between its eyes!

A flounder's eyes move, but it takes a long time. And it only happens once in the fish's lifetime. When the flounder is small, it looks like any other fish. It has one eye on each side of its head.

But as the flounder grows, something strange begins to happen. One eye very slowly moves across the flounder's head toward the other side of its face. Eventually, both eyes are on one side. The flounder (left) spends its adult life lying on the ocean bottom with its "eye side" up.

The eyes of the conch (KAHNK) and the ghost crab are at the end of movable stalks. The conch (right) is like a big snail. It can pull its eyes back into the protection of its big, heavy shell. The ghost crab (below) hides in the sand with just its eyes sticking out. It is safe from predators but can still watch for prey.

Our eyes are built for one *habitat,* or kind of place. We live on land and usually go in the water for short periods of time. Some animals spend lots of time both on land and in the water. They must have eyes that work in both places.

Crocodiles sometimes hunt by floating in the water. Hippopotamuses like to cool off in the water during the heat of the day. Both of these animals have eyes near the top of their head. They can still see even when they are almost completely under water. The hippo watches for danger. The crocodile looks for prey.

The unusual fish *Anableps anableps* (ANNA–bleps) is nicknamed the "four–eyed fish." It really only has two eyes. But each eye is divided into two parts. *Anableps* often lies just at the water's surface. It can watch out for seabirds flying in the sky above it and hunt for fish in the water below it—at the same time!

Mudskippers (above) are strange fish. They spend hours out of the water sitting on the roots of mangrove trees! Their bulging, movable eyes work well underwater. Out of water, they can only see things that are very close.

WHEN YOU DON'T NEED EYES

Some animals live their whole life with only limited eyesight or none at all. There are animals that have lived for many, many generations in dark caves. Because they didn't need their eyes, these animals have gradually lost them completely. When they are very young, blind cave fish have eyes. But the eyes disappear as the fish grows older.

Moles spend most of their life tunneling through the ground, searching for food. They don't see very well. Sometimes their eyes are even covered over with skin. Moles can tell light from dark. But they rely much more on touch and smell to find prey and get around.

Earthworm eyes are just a group of light–sensitive cells covered with a jellylike substance. An earthworm can tell dark from light. It can also tell from where the light is coming. Even if an earthworm's eyes are covered, it can still sense brightness. The earthworm's whole body is light–sensitive.

We say someone is "blind as a bat." But bats aren't really blind. Some see as well as other mammals their size.

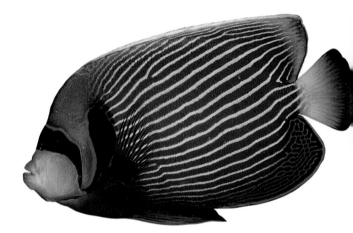

COLORS

SO MANY COLORS!

People come in different colors. Our hair, eyes, and skin can all be different from those of our friends. But animals come in many more colors and patterns than people.

This tree frog has lots of colors. It even has red eyes and orange toes! But when the tree frog rests, it sits with its eyes closed. Then the bright colors are hidden, and the green frog blends in with the tree in which it sits.

If something startles the frog, it opens its eyes and moves. This sudden flash of bright colors can scare a predator, and give the frog time to escape.

58

Some animals show very little color. You can almost see right through the ghost catfish below. It is transparent (trans-PAIR-ent). Transparent animals are hard for their enemies to see.

The uakari (wah-KAH-ree) is a monkey. Like most monkeys, the uakari is covered with hair. But its face is red and has almost no hair on it. When a uakari gets excited or upset, its face gets even brighter red.

WATCH OUT!

People sometimes use colors to give a warning. Signs that are bright orange or red tell us to be careful. Animals use warning colors, too!

The gila (HEE-la) monster isn't really a monster. It's a lizard. Gila monsters live in the deserts of Mexico and the United States. Their bite is poisonous. The gila monster's orange and black markings serve as a warning to stay away.

There are many kinds of poison dart frogs in South America. They have very colorful markings. The bright colors warn other animals that the frogs are poisonous. Native people apply the poison that comes from the skin of these frogs to darts and arrowheads for hunting small animals.

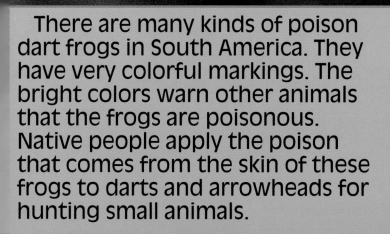

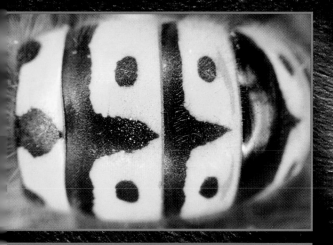

Like this hornet, flying insects that sting are often yellow and black. Think of the bumblebee. Some harmless insects are also yellow and black. By looking like the insects that sting, they are protected from predators.

Mandrills are a kind of baboon. They live in groups. Scientists who have watched mandrills think that the male's bright colors help to tell other mandrills that he is in charge.

PRESTO CHANGE-O!

Color in our skin comes from pigment. Some animals change color by changing pigments in their skin or hair. Certain animals can change color whenever they want. Others change automatically when it's the right time.

The chameleon (kuh-MEAL-ee-un) is a lizard that changes color as its mood changes. It also changes color to send messages to other chameleons, or to blend in with its environment. Colors or patterns that blend in with the background are called camouflage (CAM-o-flahj).

The octopus can turn many different colors. You can see the colors changing as you watch. The octopus has special, colored parts of its skin that it can make bigger or smaller within moments to hide itself on the seafloor.

Some animals change colors when the seasons change. They are white in winter to blend with snow, and brown in summer to mix with the forest floor. This weasel is partway through its seasonal change. It may take several weeks to change all the way.

63

GROWING UP

Our hair gets grayer as we get older. But our skin stays almost the same color our whole lives. Many baby animals are colored very differently than their grown-up relatives. Sometimes it is hard to tell they are the same kind of animal.

You would never guess that these are both emperor angelfish. The young fish has circles and spots. The adult has completely different markings and a cool black mask.

A baby Brazilian tapir is striped and spotted like a watermelon! As it gets older, the light marks will slowly go away. Then it will be plain brown all over, just like its mom and dad.

These birds are both bald eagles. The young, brown bird won't get its yellow beak, white head, and white tail feathers until it is four or five years old. That's when it will be grown-up.

SPOTS AND STRIPES

We are generally the same color all over. Some animals are like this, too. But other animals are covered in stripes, spots, and strange and colorful patterns.

A tiger's orange fur has bold black stripes. The tiger is easy to see in the open. But when tigers are hunting, their stripes help them to hide. The stripes look like the patterns made by shadows of trees and long grass.

Why does this clown shrimp have big purple spots? This could confuse an animal that's looking for food. The shrimp may not match the predator's idea of a meal. Markings that make an animal's shape hard to detect are called disruptive (dis-RUP-tiv) coloring.

The bright stripes of this racer snake actually help it to hide. The light and dark lines break up the snake's shape, making it hard to see the snake slithering through grass.

It's not certain why giraffes are spotted. When giraffes are feeding in a grove of trees, their spots may make them harder for lions to see. Their markings blend in with the spots of light that filter through leaves. On the plains, giraffes are easy to see. But *they* can see long distances, too. They can see predators coming, and run away.

BOYS AND GIRLS

In people, boys and girls have the same kind of coloring. But in some species of animals, males and females look very different.

If you have pet guppies, you may be wondering why some are more colorful than others. With some kinds of guppies, you can tell the males and females apart by their tails. Male guppies have fancy markings and colors on their tails. The females are less colorful.

Male frigatebirds have a bright red pouch on their throat. They puff their pouch with air and make noises when they are trying to attract a female. Once a male has a mate, the red color of his pouch starts to fade.

Female peacocks are called peahens. They are mostly gray and brown. But male peacocks have spectacular colors hidden in their big tail. The male opens his tail like a fan to get a female's attention.

If you're a relative of the monkey known as a black lemur, it's easy to tell if you're a female or a male. Just look at your fur! If it's jet black, you're a male. Black lemurs with brown fur are females.

BRILLIANT BIRDS

Compared to birds, people aren't very colorful. There is a good reason. Birds have the best eyes of any animal when it comes to seeing colors. Birds often rely on color to attract a mate.

Parrots are some of the world's most colorful birds. Many are green, blue, and yellow. This scarlet macaw also has bright, glowing red feathers. Imagine seeing these birds flying over their Amazon rain forest home!

Most birds have brightly colored feathers. But the toucan (TOO-can) can have a rainbow of colors on its beak. Different kinds of toucans have different-colored beaks.

The blue of this malachite (MAL-uh-kite) kingfisher doesn't come from a colored pigment in its feathers. The color is made by light passing through the feathers. This is the same kind of color you see on a soap bubble or an oily water puddle.

Quetzals (ket-SULS) live in Central American rain forests. Their brilliant green feathers were prized and traded by the ancient Maya (MY-uh) people. A quetzal's green tail may grow to 30 inches long!

IN BLACK AND WHITE

Many animals are brightly colored. But there are also animals that are plain black or white. Some are both black and white.

Sometimes this animal is called a black panther. It is really a black leopard. You can see its spots. Instead of yellow with black spots, it is all black because its fur is colored by the pigment melanin (MELL-uh-nin). Melanin is the same pigment that gives our skin its unique color.

The beluga is a white whale that lives in northern oceans. Baby belugas are pale pink when they are born. They gradually turn brown, then dark bluish gray. This color slowly gets lighter. The beluga is finally white when it is about seven years old.

Zebras are easy to recognize, with their black and white stripes. Scientists aren't sure why they have such bold markings. The stripes may break up the zebra's outline and make it harder for predators to see. Or they may help zebras to recognize each other.

This gray squirrel is completely white because it's an albino (al-BY-no). Albinos don't have any melanin to darken their skin and fur. Albinos also have pink eyes because they don't have any pigment to hide the blood that runs through them.

73

BORROWED COLORS

Some animals get their colors in a strange way. The colors don't appear naturally. Often, they come from outside sources such as plants and food.

Sloths are slow-moving animals. They hang from trees in South American rain forests. Their long fur sometimes looks green, but it didn't grow that way. The color comes from tiny plants called algae (AL-jee). The plants live on the sloth's fur.

Wild flamingoes are bright pink. The color comes from pigments in the algae and plankton the flamingoes eat. These are the same pigments that give carrots and tomatoes their color. Flamingoes in zoos sometimes lose their color. But if they are given the right kind of food, they will turn pink again.

The part of this giant clam sticking out between the top and bottom shell is called a mantle. It is very brightly colored. But don't be fooled! The clam's color comes from tiny blue and green algae living in the mantle.

75

UNDER THE SEA

Some of the most colorful animals in the world live in a coral reef.

A reef is made by millions of very small animals called coral polyps (POL-ips). These brightly colored corals provide background for animals that live near the reef. See the red fish swimming around the red coral?

Anemones (uh-NEM-oh-nees) are animals that look like plants. The parts that look like petals are really stinging tentacles. A fish swimming too close will get stung. Then the tentacles pull the fish into the anemone's stomach.

The most extraordinary colors on the reef might belong to the nudibranch (NUDE-uh-brank). Nudibranchs are like snails without shells. They move through water by fluttering the edges of their bodies.

BLAH BLAH

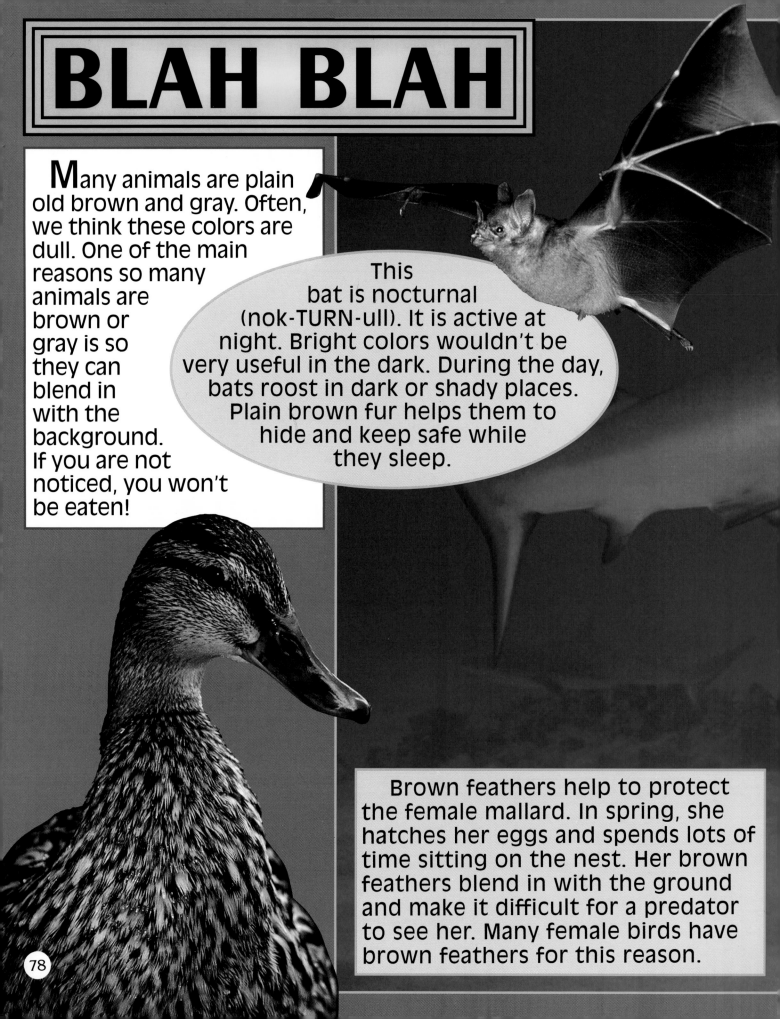

Many animals are plain old brown and gray. Often, we think these colors are dull. One of the main reasons so many animals are brown or gray is so they can blend in with the background. If you are not noticed, you won't be eaten!

This bat is nocturnal (nok-TURN-ull). It is active at night. Bright colors wouldn't be very useful in the dark. During the day, bats roost in dark or shady places. Plain brown fur helps them to hide and keep safe while they sleep.

Brown feathers help to protect the female mallard. In spring, she hatches her eggs and spends lots of time sitting on the nest. Her brown feathers blend in with the ground and make it difficult for a predator to see her. Many female birds have brown feathers for this reason.

The pale gray of the shark blends with the color of the ocean. Many fish are gray, silver, or blue for this reason. The color of a shark's skin makes it hard for prey to see the shark approaching.

Elephants are big! They don't need to be a bright color to be noticed. And camouflage spots won't really help them to hide. Plain gray works very well for the elephant.

Photo Credits

Stephen Frink: pages 94, 95
Glen & Rebecca Grambo: page 92
Breck P. Kent: pages 87, 90-91, 98, 101
Steven J. Krasemann: page 90
Dwight Kuhn: pages 93, 98-99, 105
Zig Leszczynski: pages 89, 104, 104-105
Robert & Linda Mitchell: page 93
Dan Nedrelo: page 95
A. B. Sheldon: pages 91, 97, 103
Norbert Wu: pages 86, 98, 103
Hal Beral/Visuals Unlimited: page 99
Dave B. Fleetham/Visuals Unlimited: pages 88-89
Barbara Gerlach/Visuals Unlimited: page 101
William Grenfell/Visuals Unlimited: page 103
Ken Lucas/Visuals Unlimited: pages 94-95
Jim Merli/Visuals Unlimited: pages 96-97, 103
Glenn M. Oliver/Visuals Unlimited:pages 82, 88, 89
Kjell B. Sandved/Visuals Unlimited: page 87
Tom Ulrich/Visuals Unlimited: page 85
Martin Harvey/The Wildlife Collection: pages 83, 84-85
Henry H. Holdsworth/The Wildlife Collection: pages 82-83
Chris Huss/The Wildlife Collection: page 84
Tim Laman/The Wildlife Collection: page 95
Gary Schultz/The Wildlife Collection: pages 100-101
Jack Swenson/The Wildlife Collection:page 87
Tom Vezo/The Wildlife Collection: page 102

DEFENSES

DEFENDING YOUR LIFE

For most animals, life is full of danger. One of the biggest threats is an attack from another animal. To avoid becoming someone's prey, animals use defenses.

The starfish will sacrifice one of its arms to an attacker. It does this to gain time to escape. Eventually, the starfish will grow a new arm to take the place of the one it gave away.

Armadillos rely on armor. They are covered with tough, flexible plates. When they are scared, armadillos curl into a ball to protect their head and stomach. Their built-in armor keeps them safe.

Prickly protection—that's what the hedgehog has. Its sharp spines are actually special hairs. The hedgehog rolls into a tight ball to cover its unprotected areas. When it does this, the skin stretches and makes the spines stick out.

Many animals run away from danger. This kangaroo's strong hind legs will carry it quickly away from trouble.

SAFETY IN NUMBERS

Traveling in a group can be a lifesaver for animals.

Some kinds of birds live in large groups. They often do this when they are raising their young. With so many others around, a bird has less chance of being the one that a predator eats.

Many kinds of fish live in groups called schools. Schools of fish move together almost like they are one big animal. The movements of the school can be confusing to predators.

When musk oxen (MUSK OX-un) are threatened by predators like wolves, they form a circle. The calves stand in the center. The adults face outward to keep an eye on the danger. The musk oxen lower their heads so they can use their horns to defend themselves.

Animals that eat plants often live together in groups. A herd of zebras is safer than one zebra by itself. There are more eyes to watch for danger.

85

BEAT IT!

One way to escape danger is to run—or swim—away. A frightened octopus first shoots out a dark cloud of ink. At the same time the octopus turns very pale. A predator may concentrate on the dark blob of ink in front of it. Meanwhile, the octopus can slip away.

If you've ever witnessed a fish shoot out of the water and fly through the air, then you may have seen a flying fish on the run. The flying fish doesn't really fly. It swims quickly to build up speed. Then it glides through the air on its long, winglike fins.

The speedy gazelle relies on its quickness to outrun predators. A gazelle may run in a zig-zag pattern. Or it may leap straight up in the air. Gazelles have been known to jump right over an attacking lion!

When it's up against a predator, the skink just goes to pieces. Really! The skink's brightly colored tail has special weak points that break away when a predator grabs it. Suddenly the predator finds itself with a wiggling tail! The skink has scuttled away to safety. It will eventually grow a new tail.

SIZE SURPRISE!

Changing appearance is one way to escape an attack. It can scare or confuse a predator. Some animals can even make themselves *seem* too big to eat.

The pufferfish doesn't look intimidating when it's swimming around. But when it's scared, the pufferfish transforms into a round ball that's hard to swallow. It does this by filling itself with water.

To frighten its enemies, the frilled lizard acts big and tough. It opens its mouth wide, and spreads the flaps of skin on its neck. Then, standing up on its hind legs, the lizard runs!

Many toads react to danger by taking big gulps of air. This makes the toad swell up and look bigger. Some toads stand on their tiptoes to be even more scary looking.

COPY CAT

Sometimes, just looking like a dangerous animal helps to keep predators away. One of the greatest mimics (MIM-icks), or look-alikes, in the animal world is a caterpillar. At left, the caterpillar makes itself look like a snake's head. It will even strike at any-thing that comes too close!

The scarlet king snake isn't poisonous, but it looks like a snake that is—the coral snake. Each snake has the same colors. The difference is the order in which the colors appear. Red separated by yellow bands means it's a poisonous coral snake. On the harmless king snake, red is separated by black bands.

Hover flies don't carry a stinger in their tail, but they fly and behave like bees. They even eat the same foods.

91

I SMELL

Many animals make bad smells to keep predators away. Some of them have a foul goo that oozes out of their body. Other animals deliver the stink directly to the enemy!

Almost everyone knows not to get too close to a skunk! When frightened, a skunk often gives a warning by stamping its front feet or doing a handstand. After that—look out! A skunk sprays a very smelly fluid from glands near its tail. It can spray up to 10 feet.

Stink bugs like this one can leave a "stink trail" where they've been feeding. Many of these smelly insects are brightly colored. This warns predators that attacking could really raise a stink!

Any animal deciding to snack on a bombardier (bom-buh-DEER) beetle is in for an unhappy surprise. When the beetle is attacked, chemicals inside its body mix together and make a hot, stinky liquid. With a very accurate aim, the beetle points its rear end at its attacker and sprays.

93

SUITS OF ARMOR

Our skeletons are inside our bodies. A crab's skeleton is the shell on the outside of its soft body. The tough, flexible shell protects the crab. As the crab gets bigger, it outgrows, or sheds, its shell. Until its new, bigger shell hardens, the crab is not protected.

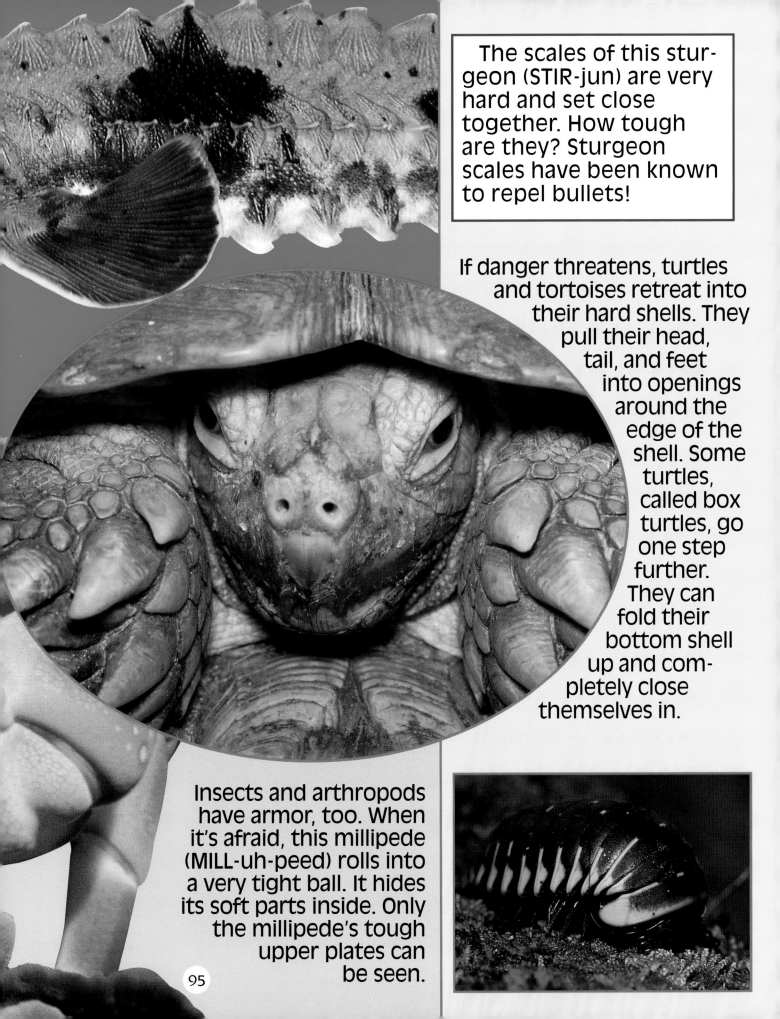

The scales of this sturgeon (STIR-jun) are very hard and set close together. How tough are they? Sturgeon scales have been known to repel bullets!

If danger threatens, turtles and tortoises retreat into their hard shells. They pull their head, tail, and feet into openings around the edge of the shell. Some turtles, called box turtles, go one step further. They can fold their bottom shell up and completely close themselves in.

Insects and arthropods have armor, too. When it's afraid, this millipede (MILL-uh-peed) rolls into a very tight ball. It hides its soft parts inside. Only the millipede's tough upper plates can be seen.

PLAYING DEAD

Many predators only like living prey. They may pause before attacking something that is already dead. So some animals play dead to fool their enemies.

When the hognose snake is threatened, it rolls over onto its back. The snake lets its mouth hang open and its tongue fall out. It lies very still. But the snake is almost too good at playing dead. If it is turned right side up, the snake flips itself back over!

96

If an opossum (uh-PAH-sum) is attacked it will fight back. If that doesn't work, the opossum "drops dead." It lies on the ground without moving, even if it is bitten by its attacker. When danger has passed, the opossum slowly gets up and scurries off.

The killdeer doesn't play dead to protect itself. But to protect its nest from a predator, the killdeer puts on an act. It pretends to be hurt and calls loudly to get the animal's attention. When it has lured the predator far enough away from the nest, the killdeer suddenly runs or flies away.

DON'T TOUCH ME

The long spines of a sea urchin are poisonous. Not many animals will try to eat a sea urchin.

Some animals use spines or stingers for protection.

When threatened, the porcupine raises its sharp quills (kwills). It keeps its quill-filled rear end pointed at the attacker. Porcupines can't throw their quills. But the quills come out of the porcupine's skin very easily. Just brushing against a porcupine can be painful.

The lionfish is beautiful but deadly. Inside its frilly fins are sharp poisonous spines. Lionfish are very easy to spot. But predators leave them alone.

The clownfish doesn't have spines, quills, or poison. But it lives with someone who does—the anemone (uh-NEM-oh-nee). Anemones look like plants but are really animals. The clownfish is protected from predators by hiding in the anemone's stinging tentacles. The sting doesn't hurt the clownfish though. The clownfish has a layer of slime on its body that protects it from the anemone.

YOU CAN'T SEE ME

You can't eat what you can't find. That's why many animals use camouflage (CAM-o-flahj) to hide. By blending into the background, they make it hard for predators to see them.

Deer fawns hide from danger by standing or lying very still. The white dots on their coat look like the spotty light coming through the trees or grass. In this field, a fawn's spots blend in very well with the clover blossoms around it.

These white ptarmigan (TAR-mi-gun) are hard to see in the snow. Only their black eyes and beaks show. When they tuck their heads under their wings, they seem to disappear. In the summer, ptarmigan turn brown to blend in with the ground and trees.

This dead leaf has eyes! Actually, the "leaf" is a butterfly's wing. By resembling the dead leaves around it, the butterfly can hide from predators. Its wings even have spots that look like bugs have been feeding on them.

You might look right at this caterpillar and never know it was there. Some caterpillars hide by looking just like part of a plant. It would take a very sharp-eyed bird to spot this one!

YUCK!

Lovely to look at, yucky to eat! Some animals are poisonous or just taste bad. A predator who has never seen one of these animals may try to eat it. But after the first time— no way! The bright colors of these bad-tasting animals warn off the predator.

The monarch (MON-ark) butterfly is bright orange and black. Those colors warn hungry birds to leave the monarch alone. Birds know that monarchs taste bad.

Usually, this toad keeps its green side up. But when it's scared, it lives up to its name—fire-bellied toad. The toad flips onto its back and shows off its bright red-and-black underside. Predators know to leave this poisonous toad alone.

Predators who try to eat the nudibranch (NUDE-uh-brank) get two surprises. Not only does the nudibranch taste bad, but it can sting, too.

This caterpillar doesn't just taste icky. Those sharp, pointy bristles will give an attacker a bad rash. Birds and other predators avoid caterpillars that look like this.

FIGHTING BACK

When some animals are threatened, they don't run away. They fight back! Claws, teeth, antlers, and tusks can all be used as weapons.

Very few people would want to argue with either of these animals. Both the Cape buffalo and the warthog are very good at defending themselves. Cape buffaloes may weigh a ton, and they seem to have bad tempers. They will charge at almost anything that moves, including lions! Warthogs often run from danger. But when they are cornered, they will fight back with their sharp tusks.

104

Rattlesnakes would rather run away than fight. But if they have to fight, they are well armed. Their poisonous fangs can deliver a dangerous bite. Rattlesnakes get their name from the noise they make by vibrating the end of their tail. Sometimes they make this noise as a warning before they strike, but not always.

In every group of termites, there are soldiers—termites with big, strong jaws. These termites are in charge of guarding the rest of the group from enemies like ants. The soldiers protect the entrances to their home. They also protect other termites who are out gathering food.

Glossary

albino: an animal that has no pigment in its skin or hair.

algae: several types of tiny, simple plants that often live in water.

Anableps anableps: the "four-eyed fish," able to see above and below water simultaneously.

anemone: a sea animal that has a soft, tubelike body and a central mouth surrounded by tentacles.

baleen: the bristly plates hanging from the jaws of certain whales that are used to filter food.

binocular vision: vision that combines the image received by each eye to create a three-dimensional picture.

bombardier beetle: a beetle that "bombs" its victims with a stinky liquid.

camouflage: a color, shape, or pattern intended to hide or disguise.

canine: in mammals, the tooth between the incisors and the molars. Canine teeth are often longer or pointed.

Carcharodontosaurus: a dinosaur that had eight-inch teeth and a six-foot-long head.

carnivore: a meat-eater.

chameleon: a type of lizard whose skin changes color.

compound eye: an eye that has several lenses; common in insects.

conch: a type of soft-bodied sea animal protected by a spiral shell. Like its relative the snail, the conch moves on a single foot.

coypu: a type of rodent that has webbed feet and lives in South America.

Deinonychus: a dinosaur that had a huge claw on its second toe.

disruptive: something that interrupts or breaks up the expected pattern.

facets: the lenses in an insect's compound eye.

gila monster: a type of large, poisonous lizard that has pink or beige and black markings.

habitat: where an animal naturally lives in the wild.

incisors: in mammals, the sharp center teeth used to tear food.

mandibles: jaws or their equivalent, especially in insects.

Maya: a group of people who have lived in Mexico and Guatemala for centuries.

melanin: a pigment found in skin and hair.

millipede: a type of arthropod that has a hard covering, segmented body, and a pair of legs at each segment.

mimics: looks or behaves like something else.

monarch butterfly: an orange and black butterfly.

musk ox: a large ox that has a thick, shaggy coat and lives in the cold northern regions of North America and Greenland.

narwhal: a type of whale that has a single, long tusk.

nautilus: a sea animal related to the octopus but protected by a spiral shell.

nictitating membrane: a very thin layer, as of skin, that covers and protects the eye.

nocturnal: active at night.

nudibranch: a soft-bodied, often colorful, sea animal related to snails.

nymph: in certain insects, the stage of development before adulthood. The nymph looks very different from the adult and may even be larger.

opossum: a mammal whose young develop and nurse inside a pouch on the female's belly.

osprey: a type of bird that catches fish.

paralyze: to immobilize a person or animal by disabling its nerves or muscles.

pigment: a substance that gives color.

polyps: in coral, the soft, hollow, tube-shaped animals that live in a coral reef and secrete the substance that forms the reef.

predator: an animal that lives by hunting other animals.

prey: an animal that is hunted by another animal for food.

ptarmigan: a type of bird living in the arctic regions. In winter, its feathers are white; in summer, they are brown

pupil: the dark opening in the center of the eye through which light passes.

quetzal: a brilliant green-and-red bird living in the forests of Central America.

quills: the stiff spines in the fur of a hedgehog or porcupine.

serrated: having a toothed edge, like a saw.

sturgeon: a type of large fish covered with bony plates.

toucan: a large, colorful bird with a large bill living in the forests of tropical Central and South America.

Tyrannosaurus: a large, meat-eating dinosaur.

uakari: a type of monkey that has a red face.

Index